Guidelines for
Reference and

on

Public

5/04

10/01/05

SERVICES GROUP

SURREY
COUNTY COUNCIL
Community Services

Library Association Publishing
London

Published by
Library Association Publishing
7 Ridgmount Street
London WC1E 7AE

Library Association Publishing is wholly owned by The Library Association.

British Library Cataloguing in Publication Data
A catalogue record for this book is available from the British Library.

ISBN 1-85604-350-9

Typeset in 13/15pt Garamond and Humanist 521 by Library Association Publishing.
Printed and made in Great Britain by Print in Black, Midsomer Norton, Somerset.

ing results
- quality inspections and audits
- Desk research using
  - statistics
  - comparison against published surveys and especially against similar or neighbouring authorities
  - benchmarking.

1.10 Examples of survey parameters

- numbers and types of visitor
- patterns of use, times of the year, week and day
- use of stock, equipment, hardware, software, facilities, Internet, online sources
- number of enquiries
- method of enquiry: in person, telephone, letter, fax, e-mail
- subject requests
- number of interlibrary loans
- number and nature of enquiries requiring staff assistance
- success of users wholly or partially finding information for themselves
- use of one or more services
- degree of satisfaction with answers to enquiries
- satisfaction with response times, for example, service delivery, answering personal enquiries, telephone answering and written communications
- degree of satisfaction with customer care.

1.11 Useful comparisons

- cost of service and staff per 1000 head of population compared with other departments and local authorities
- expenditure on resources per 1000 head of population compared with other departments and local authorities
- performance against advertised standards; for example, the number of hours actually open compared with those advertised.

1.12 Cautions

Be very clear about what this information will and will not reveal and remember:

> There are three kinds of organisations:
> those that make things happen;
> those that watch things happen;
> those that wonder what happened.
>
> Anon.

2 The information service

Introduction

Once the community's particular information needs are understood, current authority policy may be used to develop the aims and objectives for the authority's information services. In this chapter 2.1 and 2.2 provide detailed templates for an information service strategy and, particularly, for its aims and objectives.

The main interface between a reference and information service and the community is the public enquiry service; 2.3 to 2.8 define principles and practice for running such a service.

The information service

2.1   Information service strategy

The strategy for an information service may usefully be set out in the form of a mission statement and a series of related aims. These lead to a series of objectives for the various parts of the service.

Mission

To provide, without bias or discrimination, an accessible information service responsive to the needs and interests of those who live, work, study or visit in the area.

Aims

To provide:

- local access across the whole of the library authority area to a coordinated, integrated and responsive information network
- public access points that utilize all appropriate media, resources and technology, and that are physically arranged to suit the effective use of the new media
- a service that is available to all members of the community regardless of age, gender, sexual orientation, race, creed or ability
- a service that reflects the users' cultural, educational, leisure, social and work needs
- a high quality general public information and referral service
- a service that is tightly focused and managed using resource selection policies, service provision standards and performance criteria
- a service that people living, working or studying in the local authority area regard as the first and obvious point of call for information.

Rationale: libraries as sources for information

A statutory requirement under the 1964 Public libraries Act is that libraries should be freely accessible for everyone who lives, works or studies in a local authority area.

The principle that all citizens should have access to information as of right is naturally of vital importance in a democratic society. The library service's contribution to this ideal is to make available, in the public domain, as wide a range of information as possible.

Reference and information services do not require their users to be registered 'members' (unlike lending services). The library does not ask who enquirers are or why they want the information.

It is important that the freedom for anyone, as of right, to use public information services, without any questions being asked, is maintained.

Libraries play a vital role in the provision of information to users because:

- they are part of a much larger network: regional, national and international
- they are open longer than other public offices: during the day, evenings, Saturdays and, in some cases, on Sundays
- they are seen as focal points within their individual local communities
- users can use them on a self-service basis and without an appointment
- they act as an easy route into the maze of bureaucracy
- they provide access to materials people would be unable to afford
- they are an independent resource: neutral, non-threatening, user-friendly, non-discriminating
- they provide a relaxed environment.

2.2 Information service objectives

2.2.1 Policy objectives

The reference and information service should provide a clear management policy for all their services and collections by:

- producing statements of purpose and setting targets
- producing collection criteria to cover selection, acquisition, access, storage and retention
- implementing a monitoring system to keep abreast of changing user demands and local and national developments.

2.2.2 General reference and information service objectives

The objectives for a general reference and information service for the local authority area should include developing and maintaining:

- a general reference, referral and information service from at least one designated building run by suitably trained staff

- access and referral centres with ICT provision to internal and external services
- a basic information service at all library service points and access from these into the wider information network
- the necessary stock, services, staff skills and knowledge.

2.2.3 Special collections and services objectives

Special collections should be maintained and developed where they have a major or unique contribution to make to the public information network locally, regionally and nationally. For each collection there needs to be:

- a statement of purpose, targets and performance criteria
- exploitation and promotion of the collection
- suitably trained staff to assist users
- cooperative arrangements with other information providers in related subject areas
- medium and long-term funding plans to ensure the collection's continued maintenance and development
- cycles of continuous review to ensure systematic control of the collections
- active participation in plans to develop electronic products and access.

2.2.4 Enquiry and referral service objectives

The library service will answer enquiries received in person, by telephone, letter or electronic means at any information access point within the local authority area. To achieve this, it is necessary to:

- provide staff in sufficient numbers at clearly designated enquiry points to respond promptly for requests for information
- train staff in reference and information techniques and the use of sources
- develop a referral network to assist with enquiries that cannot be answered
- provide support and backup from the main information department to staff in other library service points.

2.2.5 Branch or community libraries and mobile library service objectives

The primary point of access to information for the majority of users will often be their branch or community library or the mobile library service. Even in the smallest service point it is therefore necessary to provide a core reference stock and ideally access to the Internet, e-mail and fax. To facilitate this, it is necessary to:

- develop and implement guidelines on the range, level and presentation of information materials in the branch or community libraries
- provide a core collection of materials at library service points dependent on defined local information profiles that should be regularly reviewed and updated

- train staff in enquiry techniques and the use of local materials
- establish efficient and effective referral systems
- provide support and guidance from specialist information services staff
- provide, wherever appropriate and available, information for people whose first language or culture is not English
- provide electronic access to facilitate access to core and/or wider information resources.

2.2.6 Local information objectives

The library authority should aim to be viewed as the major provider of current local information. To achieve this the library service should:

- lead in the collection and dissemination of information on the responsibilities and services of the local authority
- develop access to local information networks including access by electronic means
- collect, disseminate and update information about local groups, organizations, voluntary bodies, clubs and societies
- collaborate in initiatives, whether of local, national or international origin, which aim to improve the availability of information to the community.

2.2.7 Objectives for children and young people

To satisfy the information needs of children and young people there should be:

- materials in the reference and information collections in branch libraries that are attractive and accessible to children and young people
- community information materials in stock covering youth issues
- materials in the main reference and information department(s) to support the demands of the National Curriculum, BTEC, SVQs and NVQs
- information collections for parents and carers
- staff working with children and young people trained in the use and exploitation of information materials.

2.2.8 Objectives for people with disabilities

Particular consideration must be taken over the information needs of people with disabilities.

Wherever feasible, information sources should be provided that are designed for ease of access and use by people with physical disabilities and in appropriate formats for people with sensory impairments.

Equipment should be made available to facilitate the use of information materials.

Where necessary alternative locations and methods of accessing information should be offered.

Reference should be made to the relevant Library Association guidelines, such as *Library and information services for visually impaired people.*

2.2.9 Social inclusion

To further social inclusion the information service should:

- ensure that information provided is as accessible as possible and that any barriers created by range, level, coverage and presentation are removed
- provide information on opportunities for individuals to participate in work and training.

The enquiry service

2.3   General

For present purposes an enquiry may be defined as 'any question leading to the active involvement of staff in identifying and answering problems posed by library users'.

The primary point of access to information for the majority of users is the branch or community library. Each library acts as an enquiry point for the whole service.

Although a library service cannot guarantee to answer every enquiry received at every service point, the aim should be always to give some information, if only a referral, in response to the user's question.

The enquiry service should be available during all hours that the service points are open. Remote access, eg through a website, should be available wherever possible to give a service 24 hours a day, 365 days a year. This should both provide information and allow users to send enquiries.

Enquiries may be made in person, over the telephone, by letter, fax, or by other electronic means.

Libraries may wish to examine the potential for some categories of enquiries to be handled through a call centre operated centrally by their local authority.

2.4   Priorities

Every enquiry should be given the same level of attention and be answered as quickly and considerately as possible.

Each authority should set standards for telephone answering and for replying to written enquiries.

In the larger and busier reference and information service, a better service is usually possible if telephone enquiries are handled by staff who are not at the same time dealing with users actually in the library.

2.5   Restrictions on enquiries handled by libraries

Libraries give information and guidance but not advice (although this distinction is not always clear-cut). This limitation is particularly important in certain areas such as law, medicine and personal finance.

Libraries can identify sources for homework, project and other learning-based enquiries and ensure that the users know how to use the resources supplied, but they do not usually undertake any research. Learners of all ages, however, may require guidance and assistance in the research process.

Libraries answer detailed enquiries for current local information about their own locality. For other localities users should be referred to the local library concerned.

Libraries need to manage the amount of time they spend on each enquiry. Realistically they may only be able to spend between ten and fifteen minutes on each enquiry. After that enquiries must be carried on by users themselves with suitable advice from staff on resources, etc, or they may be referred to a fee-based information service.

2.6   The enquiry process

Answering an enquiry involves some or all of the following:

- putting the user at their ease
- finding out precisely what it is the user wants, how much they want, whether they have any deadlines and any preferred format
- assessing the most appropriate format or medium for the answer
- providing a specific resource or piece of information for a user
- ensuring that the enquirer knows how to use the information source (eg catalogue, index, CD-ROM)
- giving the source of any information supplied
- referring the user on to another information supplier
- checking that the user is satisfied with the outcome.

2.7   Referrals

Ideally the aim should be to answer an enquiry immediately using resources at the service point. A library will often, however, need to access the resources of another information provider or refer the enquirer to another information provider because:

- the original library does not have the materials to answer the enquiry
- the other provider may be able to offer the information in greater depth
- the other provider may be able to find the information more quickly or effectively
- the other provider may have the information in a more appropriate format
- it may be quicker or more convenient for the enquirer to visit another library

or information provider
- the other provider may have better study facilities or equipment
- the other provider may be able to offer advice as well as information.

When referring a user to another information provider, library staff need to:

- ensure that the user knows where the library, department or office is, when it is open, the phone number and how to get there
- check that the other source has the book or information needed. If it is not possible to do this immediately, the enquirer should be advised to check before making any visit
- check with the alternative source to confirm, firstly, their willingness to accept visits from the public, and then their opening hours and any other relevant information.

2.8 The role of specialist information services' staff in the public library

Within the reference or information services section trained and experienced staff should be available at all times to answer enquiries directly or to assist other staff handling enquiries.

Staff of the reference or information services section should give assistance over the telephone to staff at other service points regarding the use of materials held locally.

If appropriate, reference and information services staff should answer enquiries for other library service points by using resources held centrally or in special collections. This could take the form of information over the telephone, faxing material, supplying photocopies, electronic document delivery or explaining the need for the user to visit another library. They should also advise staff at the service points on the most appropriate alternative sources for information.

3 Information resources

Introduction

The subject of this chapter is the information materials themselves. The principles behind the selection and management of information resources is dealt with first (3.1), followed by a detailed listing of materials appropriate to each of five levels of service. These levels are defined according to the population served by the local authority (3.7).

Selection and management

3.1   Selection policy

Materials purchased for information provision must satisfy the needs of users, potential as well as actual, and this should be the prime consideration in any selection process.

All stock should reflect the information needs of the community served.

The library service should be able to provide on demand, and largely from its own resources, information on all topics of public interest and concern. Access to such information may be either from hard copy, from electronic sources or from networks.

Where information cannot be provided from its own resources, the library service should either obtain it for the client from an alternative agency, or advise the enquirer how it might be obtained. To this end, the library service needs access to basic bibliographic tools, either hard-copy or electronic, electronic catalogues and indexing and abstracting services, as well as guides to information resources, both local and national.

Each library authority should devise an appropriate selection policy for information material to satisfy the needs of the community served. Such a policy should be frequently revised to take account both of changing information needs and new information sources, whether hard-copy or electronic.

Materials should cover a wide range of levels and be suitable for all age groups in the community.

The selection policy should ensure that the needs of those with visual disabilities are met.

3.2   Methods of selection

- bookshop visits
- publishers' catalogues
- *The Bookseller*
- bibliographies

- specialist journals
- the library community's professional press, for example *Refer*
- lists of approvals
- the expertise and knowledge of the information services staff
- providers of specialist information
- CD-ROM book trade sources
- Internet.

3.3 Currency

Every library authority should set standards for currency, and no information section at any enquiry point should make available:

- resources that are substantially or misleadingly out-of-date. Particular attention should be given to science and technology, computer studies, economics, employment, management, law, education and travel
- directories and yearbooks published more than two years ago unless there is a clear justification for longer retention, eg the information is unique to a particular source
- general multi-volume encyclopaedias published more than five years ago
- loose-leaf publications that are not completely up-to-date
- any legal item that is not the latest edition
- other titles, not covered above, that are more than one edition out-of-date, unless they are used for historical or biographical purposes, or are complemented by, rather than supplanted by newer editions
- items where the presentation is dated and there are better alternatives
- items physically damaged, defaced, dirty or worn out.

Any reference book that is not the current edition should be marked with an appropriate warning label.

3.4 Weeding

It is vital that out-of-date material is removed from the shelves, even if no replacement is available. Out-dated CD-ROMs should be removed and users should be advised that some sources on the Internet may be inaccurate or not current. In primary reference libraries it is essential that adequate retrospective files of standard directories, yearbooks, encyclopaedias and biographical sources are retained. Material stored in closed access should not be forgotten. Retention policies for little-used material should be regularly reviewed and alternative storage options be explored for appropriate material.

The practice of sending previous editions of reference works to smaller information service points should be viewed with caution: currency may be improved on occasion by substituting electronic information.

3.5   Electronic information resources

3.5.1 Selection and evaluation

The rapidly changing market of electronic information sources requires information providers to keep abreast of new developments by regularly scanning media sources as well as the library and information press. The *Library Technology* supplements to the *Library Association Record*, publicity from the leading producers of electronic products, and publicity on the Internet will all be useful.

The selection criteria for electronic resources are similar to those for hard copy material with the added considerations of:

- the loading time being acceptable on the equipment the library will be using
- the title being easy for users to search provided on-screen or printed help is made available.

Decisions about replacing hard copy with electronic alternatives will also be influenced by a variety of other points, including the relative cost of the items, licence fees, hardware installation and maintenance, and the cost of replacement of printer cartridges and paper. It may be desirable to purchase an electronic alternative simply to make it more widely available within the network.

Electronic versions of products need to be evaluated in terms of both their information content, and how efficiently that information may be accessed relative to the hard copy alternative. As more information becomes available electronically and costs fall, authorities may move towards a predominantly electronic solution to information provision, particularly in small libraries. However for the foreseeable future electronic and hard-copy information sources will co-exist side by side, and the reference and information service will need to cater for both.

Finally, electronic products rarely exactly replicate their older hard copy counterparts, it is therefore important to ensure that information is not being lost before discarding key hard-copy materials that appear to have an electronic counterpart.

3.5.2 Information sources on the Internet

Within the next few years most libraries will have access to the Internet for staff and users. Indeed the Internet will become the major source for information, replacing other hard copy and electronic resources. The amount of potential information available, therefore, at even the smallest library will be enormous. The management of this situation will be complex and challenging; information from the Internet comes unselected, it cannot be weeded or deleted, details on provenance, currency or maintenance are hard to find and it is set within an environment of continuous change. Along with the information being outdated, irrelevant and impossible to authenticate, searching for it can be time-consuming and often fruitless.

The information service will need to take a proactive role as the navigator or guide to these resources by providing:

- 'bookmarks' to individual sites of interest to particular libraries or collections
- 'gateways' to sites put up by local organizations and bodies
- indexes to sites of use to different sizes of library
- links to external indexing sites, eg *EARLweb*.

When examining the potential of any source the following are some of the factors that need to be considered:

- intended audience
- accurancy and currency of content
- reliability and stability of the site
- ease of navigation and use
- speed of access
- evidence of quality control processes
- comprehensiveness – especially with journals when only part of an issue may be available
- existence of an archive
- presence of links to further sources (and whether they work).

The ultimate test for any source is its fitness for purpose and that it meets the needs of the user seeking information. Because users can access the whole range of sites available and not just those the library service has recommended or highlighted, notices must be displayed warning that information found may be inaccurate, misleading or out-of-date.

Standards for resource provision

3.6   Levels of service: categories

Standards for minimum levels of service provision depend on the size of the catchment area covered by the service. The categories are defined by population within the catchment area. The population figures refer to residential or daytime numbers, whichever is the greater:

A   Reference services serving populations above 500,000
B   Populations between 250,000–500, 000
C   Populations between 100,000–250,000
D   Populations between 25,000–100,000
E   Populations below 25,000.

Authorities without a large centre of population should consider raising the level of their provision to give users access to a reasonable reference resource particularly if there is some distance to the nearest large library.

The guidelines below describe the categories and the range of information types that are appropriate for each level of service defined above. The information is given in three sections: the first (3.7) recommends provision for libraries other than the smallest (Category E) using a subject breakdown. The second (3.8) recommends core stock for Category E libraries, and the third (3.9) notes important materials recommended for special groups of users such as the physically challenged.

For all the materials listed below, electronic format should be considered where available as a possible alternative to hard copy.

All collections will need to be supplemented or amended to meet particular local circumstances.

These guidelines are complemented by *Basic reference stock for the public library* (Library Association Information Services Group, 1998) which lists *specific titles* suitable for reference and information services with daytime or residential populations in excess of 100,000.

Standards for mobile libraries provision are set in The Library Association's *Charter for public mobile library services.*

3.7 Resource guidelines for categories A to D

Encyclopaedias

- **A** Comprehensive range of the major multi-volume encyclopaedias in English and other major languages (either electronic or hard copy).
- **B** Some major multi-volume encyclopaedias, single volume works in major languages, in addition to titles listed in *Basic reference stock.*
- **C –D** All titles listed in *Basic reference stock.*

Language dictionaries

- **A** The major national monolingual dictionaries (either in electronic or hard copy) of all major languages, especially those of the European Union; general dictionaries in print listed in *Walford's guide to reference material*; a wide range of specialist subject translating dictionaries.
- **B** The selection should reflect the cultural environment served and should include monolingual dictionaries for major languages at the level of the *Shorter Oxford dictionary*, and bilingual dictionaries at the level of *Harrap's standard French and English dictionaries*; a selection of special subject translating dictionaries, in addition to all titles listed in *Basic reference stock.*
- **C–D** All titles listed in *Basic reference stock.*

| Catchment population key | **A** >500,000 | **B** 250–500,000 | **C** 100–250,000 |
| | **D** 25–100,000 | **E** <25,000 | |

Directories, guides and business information sources

- **A** All telephone directories, both alphabetical and yellow pages, for the British Isles, Western Europe and the principal trading centres of the world. UK postal address books, and those of the European Union and major overseas countries (where available). The majority of directories listed in *Current British directories*; a comprehensive range of general commercially published foreign trade directories, commercial business information services for British and foreign countries; company annual reports, market research reports and trade catalogues.
- **B** All telephone directories, both alphabetical and yellow pages, for the British Isles, the major cities of the European Union and major trading partners. UK postcode directories; general trade directories for the UK's principal trading partners; a wide range of British specialized professional and trade directories; the principal hard copy and electronic information sources on the top 1000 British companies. Market research reports. Information on local companies and trade companies. Guidebooks for European countries and major tourist centres of the world.
- **C** All titles listed in *Basic reference stock.*
- **D** All telephone and postal address books for the British Isles; local directories; a limited range of UK trade and professional directories to meet local needs; guides for major tourist areas, British and foreign.

Periodicals including newspapers

A–C The selection of titles should reflect the cultural, economic and social needs of the community being served. A minimum of 100–250 titles, including indexes to general periodicals and newspapers, with a range of British national, local and community newspapers. Internet access may also be provided for current material. Files of adequate length should be maintained, bearing in mind the availability of files in other libraries.

A (additionally) All British national and relevant regional newspapers of substantial information content, together with all local newspapers. Major foreign newspapers.

D A selection of British national and local newspapers.

Maps and plans

A–D All 1:50,000 Ordnance Survey maps; 1:25,000 Ordnance Survey maps for local counties (or 25 mile radius); all maps for area within local authority boundary (strategies must be developed to ensure that archival copies of large-scale digital maps, eg 1:10,000, are retained); local Geological Survey 1:50,000 maps;

Catchment population key   **A** >500,000   **B** 250–500,000   **C** 100–250,000
                                      D 25–100,000   **E** <25,000

Ordnance Survey Historical maps; all street plans for local towns and major British cities; local transport maps. Foreign Hallweg or similar maps for Europe; street plans for major overseas tourist centres.

A (additionally)   Comprehensive collection of UK town guides and maps; Geological Survey 1:50,000 maps for Great Britain; 1:10,500 maps for the region, complete sets of Soil Survey and Land Utilisation maps; Admiralty charts according to local demand. There should be electronic access to digital mapping facilities.

A–C   Comprehensive collection of UK town guides and maps; street plans for major cities of the world. 1:100,000 for Ireland.

Timetables

- **A–D**   All titles listed in *Basic reference stock.* These should include bus and rail services in the area served by the library, as well as national coach, bus and rail timetables.

Official publications

- **A–B**   Individual Public General Acts and *Halsbury's Statutes of England*; individual statutory instruments and *Halsbury's Statutory Instruments*; Hansard (Commons and Lords) daily (unless Internet access is available); other official publications on matters of special public concern.
- **C–D**   Individual Public General Acts (or *Halsbury's Statutes of England*); cumulated volumes of statutory instruments; Hansard (Commons and Lords) weekly (unless Internet access is available); other official publications on matters of special public concern.
- **A** (additionally)   All Stationery Office publications; European Union publications; selected publications of the United Nations and its agencies; selected publications of the OECD and other international organizations, and foreign governments. Access may be via the Internet but permanent files will be necessary for many of these publications.

European Union

Each library authority should be a member of the European Public Information Relay (PIR) and abide by the agreement made with the London Office of the European Commission. Members should conform to the three-tier system established between the Commission Office and the Society of Chief Librarians or any subsequent system and follow any recommended stock holding lists produced:

- **A**   Tier One

Catchment population key	**A** >500,000 **B** 250–500,000 **C** 100–250,000
	D 25–100,000 **E** <25,000

- **B–C** Tier Two
- **D** Tier Three

Statistics

- **A–D** As a minimum all titles cited in *Basic reference stock*, plus statistical publications of local interest.
- **A** (additionally) All British official statistical publications; all statistical publications of the European Union and the OECD; and a wide range of statistical publications of the United Nations and other international organizations; a wide range of foreign statistical publications, including all official statistical yearbooks of principal trading countries.

Standards and specifications

- **A** Complete set of British Standards (BSI) including Codes of Practice; selected indexes, lists and guides to other British and foreign standards.
- **B–D** *BSI Yearbook.*

Patents

- **A–D** Information providers should be aware of the location of patents.

Bibliographies

- **A–D** In addition to titles listed in *Basic reference stock*, libraries in categories A and B should have access to the *British National Bibliography, Global Bookbank Plus,* or *Bookfind,* as well as principal indexing and abstracting services such as *British Humanities Index,* and Stationery Office catalogues and bibliographies from major foreign countries and international organizations. A wide range of library catalogues are available electronically and these should be available on demand.

Biography and genealogy

- **A–D** All titles listed in *Basic reference stock.*
- **A** (additionally) 'Who's whos' and national biographical dictionaries for major countries; specialized biographical dictionaries; and principal British genealogical sources (for example published parish registers, the International Genealogical Index, Harleian Society publications). It is expected that this material will normally fall within the remit of local studies.
- **B** Selected foreign national biographical dictionaries and 'who's whos';

Catchment population key	**A** >500,000	**B** 250–500,000	**C** 100–250,000
	D 25–100,000	**E** <25,000	

major British genealogical sources (for example published parish registers, the International Genealogical Index, Harleian Society publications).

Local material

- **A–D** A representative selection of local material reflecting the local and historical needs of the community. Reference should be made to *Local studies libraries: Library Association guidelines for local studies provision in public libraries* (second edition in preparation).

Community information

- **A–D** This should reflect the social, economic, educational and cultural needs of the community served. Besides the basic book stock there should also be leaflets available for the public to take away (these may be acquired through services such as *FRILS* – Free Information Leaflet Suppliers) covering health, taxation and welfare and benefits. The collection should include current information about local authorities, local organizations, local events, local transport, local electoral registers, local street maps, guides and directories. Current guides to the law, and career guides and educational prospectuses should be provided. The selection must reflect local community needs and should be available in the languages of the local community wherever possible.

3.8   Core resources for the smallest libraries (category E)

Community and consumer information

- Current information about local authorities, local organizations, local events, local transport, local electoral registers, local street maps, guides and directories; Ordnance Survey 1:50,000 maps including the area covered by the library, minutes of local councils, local telephone directories, local postal address book, basic guides to the law, career guides and educational prospectuses; consumer information (for example *Which?*), plus leaflets on health, benefits, taxation, etc, which should be in languages of the community served by the library.

General information

- multi-volume encyclopaedia
- yearbook (for example *Whitaker's almanack*)
- book of facts
- guide to the law
- English language dictionary

Catchment population key	**A** >500,000	**B** 250–500,000	**C** 100–250,000
	D 25–100,000	**E** <25,000	

- bi-lingual dictionaries in the major European languages and languages spoken in the community served by the library
- dictionary or encyclopaedia of science and technology
- medical dictionary
- dictionary of quotations
- bus, coach and rail timetables
- world atlas and gazetteer
- British road atlas and gazetteer
- 1:50,000 Ordnance Survey local sheet, atlases and street maps for local area
- European Information: Public Information Relay binder

3.9 Resources for specific needs

This section covers the needs of special groups of users. It is an indicative rather than a comprehensive list and serves to highlight the importance of considering special requirements. Some of the groups are covered by Library Association guidelines: they are available for services for children and young people, mobile library users, services for housebound people, local studies provision and prison libraries. Details of the individual publications may be found in the bibliography.

The lists below are categorized by types of special need:

- Students of all types
  - study space
  - computer facilities
  - electronic sources
  - guides to courses, qualifications and financial support

- Employees
  - employment opportunities and careers
  - job advertisements
  - information on writing job applications and curriculum vitae
  - information on succeeding at interview
  - information on employers
  - employees rights
  - guides to working abroad

- Leisure
  - what's on: locally and nationally
  - contact names and addresses
  - records of achievement (for example in sport)

- For everyday living
  - services of local and central government
  - consumer information
  - electoral register
  - information on the political process, elections, constituencies, wards
  - health information including self-help and support groups

- Aids to access
  - magnifying equipment, software, text enhancement, enlarging photocopy facilities
  - large-print materials, user notices
  - talking newspapers, books, magazines, taped information
  - information on equipment, holidays, benefits, rights, care for people
- Ethnic groups
  - first language materials for ethnic groups
  - information and newspapers on cultural, religious and ethnic issues
  - English-as-a-second-language courses.
- Social inclusion
  - information on opportunities to participate in work and learning
  - details of community and social initiatives
  - sources of literacy and numeracy advice and guidance
  - health and environmental information.

4 Information and communication technology (ICT)

Introduction

The addition of information technology products and systems to information services has introduced many new opportunities but also some new challenges. ICT is often difficult to deal with because of the hype and mystique surrounding the technology, the lack of experience of many people in using the systems (compounded by the pace of development of the services themselves) and the complex nature of some of the software needed to access them.

Nevertheless it is essential that the new opportunities for information access are made available to the public and that staff are properly trained in utilizing the technology. Staff also need to be trained to explain to users how the equipment and software works and to demonstrate how the information potential of the services may be achieved.

ICT services

4.1 ICT in the public information service

New Library: the people's network argues for 'the transformation of libraries and what they do . . . for re-equipping them and reskilling their staff so that they can continue to fulfil their widely valued role as intermediary, guide, interpreter and referral – but now helping smooth the path to the technological future'.

It is clear today that many types of information are already more cost-effective to purchase in an ICT format or to access using ICT, and this trend looks set to continue.

ICT provides big advantages for information services who have to operate from many geographically separated sites. Greater concentrations of expertise are possible at central sites, and greater levels of information are available at branch sites. ICT will increasingly be necessary to access government and other public information.

It is difficult to be confident about exactly what will happen or when, but perhaps the greatest long term impact of ICT on public information services is that information provision will no longer be as limited as it is at present by the physical constraint of distance. In the long term this may mean a reduction in the use of public information services by some groups, but past experience strongly suggests that many sections of society will continue to need and will expect the public library service to provide a focus for information in ICT formats together with expertise on how it should be used.

Meanwhile, public libraries, with their wide geographical spread and their remit for providing information to the public, are uniquely placed to provide public access to the information superhighways. The current availability of ICT systems and services enables libraries to:

- provide a network encompassing all service points that responds quickly to requests for information
- provide users with access to a greater range of materials – locally, nationally and internationally
- improve access to catalogues and indexes
- improve access to information for disadvantaged members of the community
- improve services for local business which can benefit from access to more, and better quality, information than previously available.

4.2 Planning

The development of ICT is expensive and many applications have implications for other parts of the library service:

- in terms of compatibility of software and hardware for wider use in the service
- because of the need for networking and the integration of systems
- because there are common training issues.

ICT planning must therefore rely on teamwork. Public library ICT developments should normally include, from the planning stage, information service inputs together with those from other appropriate areas.

All strategies and plans need to be revised at least every two years.

A long term aim should be to have all electronic forms of information integrated into one seamless mode of access.

4.3 Services

In particular there are a number of specific ways in which a library service should extend its ICT work. An expanded range of information can be provided, and its availability be extended, by:

- creating a CD-ROM network to all service points and providing a wide range of titles
- providing Internet access to the public in order to give users access to more local, national and international information sources
- increasing the coverage of council and local information provision in ICT formats, for example through networks used for issue and cataloguing systems to

branch libraries
- taking part in local initiatives involving the development and exploitation of information provided in electronic form
- computerizing relevant indexes and catalogues to give improved access to information collections and services
- exploring how access to information services could be offered by private communications providers such as cable companies
- offering services in the libraries in conjunction with commercial organizations
- providing access for the business community to relevant databases such as those covering market research, legislation and careers information
- participating in the National Grid for Learning, National Digital Library, University for Industry and other similar initiatives
- being a local ICT centre which supports lifelong learning, providing access to hardware, software and networks and developing and being aware of partnerships with higher education institutions such as e-Lib and metropolitan area networks (MANS)
- fulfilling children's high expectations of computer resources and ease and speed of access to information by providing resources geared to the National Curriculum and the development of core skills
- providing access to digitized maps at all service points
- providing access electronically to as much local material as possible eg local newspapers, catalogues of local collections and digitized local studies resources
- providing an electronic document delivery service
- participating in cooperative projects such as the EARL Consortium's *Ask a Librarian*
- being more accessible to the community at large by setting up a home page for the library service on the world wide web, by developing links to other websites and by developing useful sign-posting for the web for users.

Cautions

In all cases services should provide the most cost-effective resources in the most appropriate format for the purpose and users intended.

Staff must be aware of current copyright regulations concerning the printing and downloading of information from the web and other ICT systems.

4.4   Internet access

The use of the Internet as an information source for library staff and library users is a recent development, but one which is expanding rapidly. Many staff feel overwhelmed by this vast influx of non-managed and seemingly non-manageable information. Policies, procedures and experiences are only just beginning to evolve. Fortunately there are several groups seeking to provide support and guidance on hardware, software, content and management issues.

During 1999 The Library Association will be producing a policy on filtering and access based on the premises that access to information should be unrestricted and free at the point of delivery.

The Library Association, EARL and UKOLN are already providing help and guidance in the form of workshops, policy documents, identification of search engines, creation of gateways, and so on.

How the Internet is used as an information tool is discussed in section 3.5.2 but it is clear that this whole area will need to be revisited again and again over the next few years.

ICT and staff

4.5   Staff specialisms

Many ICT issues are of a technical or specialized nature. Also the rapid changes that occur in ICT make it impractical for all staff to keep up with developments. It is therefore advisable to have suitably trained and experienced staff in each authority specifically responsible for:

- planning and managing ICT developments
- operational management of large ICT systems
- training others in ICT system use
- advice and guidance on selection of ICT software and hardware.

When recruiting new staff, it is important that they not only have the relevant knowledge and skills but also have a positive attitude to using ICT to deliver services.

4.6   Staff training

All staff supporting information work need training in ICT systems. *Building the new library network* sets out the steps needed to equip staff with these skills and abilities. Libraries should develop plans for establishing a skills base in ICT and should provide training including, where necessary, longer-term education. Plans should include provision for a programme of continuous basic ICT training covering operation of systems currently in use. Distance learning, self-instruction and manufacturers' or other commercial courses may often be appropriate.

Authorities should be aware of, and participate in, any collaborative training initiatives, such as the EARL Consortium's *Getting Trained.*

They should also look at the possibility of participating in consortium training for CD-ROMs.

Technical issues

4.7 Standards

There are as yet no formal standards in existence for reference and information services. Pending such standards, the following provides a checklist of the main issues and a few basic guidelines:

- Systems should meet recognized international standards, such as Z39.50 for server and client capabilities.
- There should be sufficient capacity in the networks used (bandwidth) for all projected ICT service provision.
- The aim should be to connect every service point within the library authority to a wide area network.
- A high level of networking and connectivity is essential and it must be possible to interface with both other internal and external systems to access and download information.
- Whilst authority wide standardization is in general recommended, there are occasions in such a fast developing field when standardization becomes too restrictive and harms service quality. For example the newest software used on CD-ROMs might not run on the standard equipment and software in use in an authority. In these circumstances flexibility is required and exceptions should be made on a controlled basis.

Once again, *Building the new library network* has some useful material, particularly in Appendix 12 on network service specifications.

4.8 Security

Files need protection against viruses. This protection must be continually used and kept up-to-date.

Any system must provide stringent validation of all data to prevent the acceptance of corrupt records. There must be full data integrity checks to ensure the security of all data held.

Other areas of risk are user access to disk drives, access to and from external networks and the physical security of the hardware. Firewalls should be in place to prevent access to sensitive information.

4.9 Budgeting

Budgeting for ICT must include the costs of hardware, technical support, staff training, software upgrades and online costs

When budgeting for hardware, sums should be allocated in forward plans for maintenance (perhaps 10% of capital value) and upgrading or replacement.

New library: the people's network suggests that the smallest library should have three to four multimedia terminals and the largest over 40.

5 Accommodation

Introduction

This chapter provides guidance on the principles behind the identification and successful use of a space within a library for reference and information use. Furniture, equipment and sign-posting are also covered.

5.1 General considerations

Users of any public reference library rightly expect the accommodation to be arranged so that:

- there is easy physical access to the information collection and adequate space in which to consult it
- the collection is well sign-posted, securely housed, and where appropriate attractively displayed
- there is well lit, quiet and comfortable space for more extended study of the collection
- access to ICT facilities is straightforward and facilities are safely housed.

Study space should be provided in all libraries, but it is recognized that this may not be possible in the very smallest branches, particularly those open 10 hours or less per week.

5.2 Stock location and access

As high a ratio as possible of stock should be available in directly accessible conditions. There should be space available near the materials to browse and take notes.

Closed-access 'stack' locations should be planned so that the material is normally accessible to users on demand at a few minutes notice. If longer delays are inevitable for whatever reason, the current waiting time should be advertised to the public with appropriate explanation.

5.3 Size of reference and information services

Members of any community should expect that:

- in libraries serving a catchment area of 100,000 people or more, separate information and study facilities are provided, in a location where convenience of access by public transport and a quiet environment are combined
- arrangements are in place for physical access to information services for any-

one; access conditions should comply with applicable sections of the Disability Discrimination Act 1995 and any subsequent legislation

- in libraries serving less than 100,000 daytime population, separate study and information facilities are provided wherever space is available
- every library has a clearly signed enquiry point which should normally be staffed
- information stock is easy to find where authorities have decided to integrate lending and reference stock.

5.4   Study space and reading areas

The amount of study space provided should be based upon local need and best value. There is an IFLA standard of 1.5 seats per 1000 daytime population but this does not take into account local pressures, availability of study facilities elsewhere in the locality and overall patterns of use.

The public working area should include space and furniture to allow consultation of large items such as maps or newspapers.

Appropriate furniture for storing and displaying newspapers and back files should be provided.

ICT workstations for both staff and public should conform to current health and safety standards, including, for example, the installation of blinds at nearby windows.

Study booths should be provided for the use of equipment where space permits.

Study space should be separate from noisy machinery, telephones, and public areas such as enquiry desks.

5.5   Furniture

Users should expect:

- furniture to conform to the current standards (e.g. BS 5459 Parts 1 and 2 for office desks and chairs)
- floor covering to be appropriate to the building and combine durability, quietness and ease of maintenance
- the top and bottom shelves to be at reasonable heights
- a tidy library: sufficient leaflet holders, carousels or other furniture should be available, so that leaflet/pamphlet material is not left loose on tables, windowsills, etc
- furniture to be kept in a good state of repair.

5.6   Equipment

Users should expect at the major reference and information centre within a local authority to have access to:

- public photocopying facilities
- a current library catalogue, preferably online
- CD-ROMs, online databases and the Internet
- word-processing facilities (with an adequate printer)
- fax transmission and receiving facilities or e-mail facilities
- microfilm and microfiche readers and reader printers.

People who are visually challenged should have access to technology that provides text enhancement for both printed and visual display presentations: at the very minimum a magnifying glass or at best a machine which converts text to spoken word. Minicom telephone systems and hearing loops should be installed where possible.

All equipment provided must be properly maintained, serviced and cleaned. Clear instructions on how to use the equipment must be displayed in the library, and staff should be available to give any additional help when required.

These resources and services should also be available at as many other libraries as possible.

5.7   Signing and display

Users should expect:

- face-out display of current periodical titles to be provided
- facilities for notice boards and display space for promotion of reference and information services and materials and use by local groups by means of leaflet display, stock display, exhibitions etc
- adequate signing in all languages relevant to that geographical area to direct users from the entrance and other parts of the libraries to the reference and information section
- reference material to be adequately marked that it is not available for loan
- clear instructions for the use of any ICT equipment to be available in plain English (and other languages, where appropriate)
- particular sections of information stock (eg business) to be adequately signed
- signs indicating which materials are not available on open access
- a plan of the library.

5.8   ICT installations

Users should find:

- electrical installations conforming to the current IEE Regulations and BS 6396
- lighting conforming to the IES Glare Index and, in practical terms, sufficient to read the title on the spine of a book on the bottom shelf in the darkest corner of the library

- directional lighting on the study tables
- a materials security system of the type that does not affect pacemakers etc
- CCTV ideally available for the protection of users as well as materials
- public access terminals to be positioned so as to conform to display screen equipment regulations in force at the time
- any equipment belonging to another agency, but housed in the library to conform to all applicable standards (eg TAPS – training access points)
- a clear indication of whether members of the public can use their own equipment such as laptop computers, and what restrictions are in force
- a statement on what restrictions are placed on the use of mobile phones in the library
- that electrical equipment is tested regularly and there are no exposed or trailing wires etc
- enough space next to terminals for a mouse to be used, if needed.

5.9   Health and safety at work

Users should expect care to be taken to conform to all national and local health and safety regulations.

The local authority's health and safety officers should be consulted as a matter of routine when making changes to buildings and they should also provide regular health and safety checks on the accommodation.

6 Management

Introduction

Most management issues in local authorities are common to all areas of the authority's varied work. This chapter discusses them from an information service perspective and covers funding (6.1), planning (6.4), staffing (6.9) and training (6.13).

Funding

6.1 Control of funding

The funding of reference and information services is usually split into three separate areas: staffing, equipment and materials.

In many authorities, staffing budgets are handled centrally and this is rarely a major concern for information services.

Equipment funding is best devolved to information service managers. The specification of the equipment required is defined directly by the software format of the information being purchased and the equipment, be it CD-ROM, microform or ICT is (although costly) ancillary to the information product itself. Any new equipment also needs to be matched to other products currently in use in the information service. Technical advice may be necessary from elsewhere in the authority, and compliance with authority standards is necessary.

Materials budgets should always be held by information services managers since they have complete responsibility for making the most cost-effective purchases.

It is helpful to retain some central coordination of information purchasing. This will maximize flexibility for occasions when special areas of the collection require inputs or when the purchase of specialized or expensive titles is desirable. Selection itself should be devolved, where appropriate, to those staff most closely involved with and knowledgeable about particular collections or services.

6.2 Funding levels

A proportion of the library authority's overall materials fund should normally be allocated specifically for the purchase of reference and information materials. The actual amount should be sufficient to implement these guidelines within an authority and maintain any additional special collections or services.

The materials allocation should include the funding for periodicals, microforms, newspapers, online access and CD-ROMs.

The availability of information in alternative media is a relatively new but increasing trend. Managers need to maintain an awareness of the factors driving current publishing and of user reactions to the use of new media, so that they can decide, in any given instance, which format will be most cost-effective.

In order to maintain proper control and to obtain realistic performance measurement, separate funding should be allocated for the support of special collections.

6.3 External funding

Purposes

Over the last decade the possibilities for obtaining external funding have increased significantly. Such funding is usually for specific projects such as the introduction of particular ICT facilities, the development of special collections or facilities for challenged groups.

Sources

Information services managers should be aware of the sources for external funding and the rules and constraints that each operate. Sources include the European Community, government challenge funds, special trusts, the National Lottery, training and enterprise councils, health authorities and collaboration with the private sector.

Planning

6.4 Statutory requirements

Under powers conferred by the 1964 Public Libraries and Museums Act, the Secretary of State requires every library authority in England to produce an annual library plan, which should follow closely the corporate strategy of the parent authority and tie in with current Government recommendations. The information services plan should form a separate and significant part of the overall library plan.

The Government guidelines issued by the Department of Culture, Media and Sport (see Bibliography) should be used to determine the format and contents of the annual library plan.

6.5 The library plan

The library plan must be divided into two linked parts:

- The medium-term plan which must:
  - be produced afresh every three years or so
  - contain an environmental analysis of the service and the community it serves

— review the overall performance of the service compared to that of other authorities
— consider the pressures faced by the service and the opportunities available to make improvements in the service to meet changing user demands
— estimate – and justify – funding implications
— describe the strategy and action plan which will be used to achieve the aims.
— indicate the methods by which performance will be measured.

- The short-term plan or rolling review which should:
  — be produced as an annual supplement to the medium-term plan
  — review progress over the last 12 months
  — analyse performance against the targets set
  — identify any additional short-term targets
  — highlight new initiatives and opportunities.

Each short-term review acts as an update and hence revision to the current medium-term plan and may well also provide significant inputs for the next medium-term plan.

6.6   Other plans

An ICT strategy should show how ICT is integrated into the overall planning and future direction of the service.

Two other plans are becoming common. One is for staff development (the purpose of which is self explanatory) and the other is usually known as a disaster plan and covers the steps to be taken to ensure continuation of services following disasters such as buildings being destroyed by fire. The creation and maintenance of these are strongly advised. They are discussed in turn below.

6.7   The staff development plan

Staff are the most valuable resource in any public service; they are also the most costly.

Maximizing their potential will always be one of a manager's major priorities. A plan to achieve this is well worth the effort involved. A staff development plan needs to:

- define the skills and experiences needed for the services
- provide a statement of how the current staff resource matches this
- include a plan to make up any shortfalls or gaps
- provide personal development plans for all staff. These should include short, medium and long term elements. Information work requires a number of skills that benefit from regular updating, notably interpersonal skills (customer care) and technical skills (information handling).

Staff development as a concept is best regarded as a long-term, ongoing process which can be effectively linked with nationally recognized standards, for example vocational qualifications (SVQs and NVQs), Investors in People (IiP) or The Library Association's Continuing Professional Development (CPD) profile. This requires planning for the developmental needs of staff in the long- or medium-term.

Training in specific areas may also be required to respond to changes in work practices, for example in connection with ICT work, and will tend to be carried out on an 'as and when' basis. A personnel appraisal system should be used by both sides to assist in identifying training needs and opportunities. Such training also needs to be linked to an individual's own long-term development.

Some sections of the staff development plan will form an integral part of the business plan but the former's greater detail will keep in focus the need to maximize the effectiveness of the services' most costly resource.

6.8 The disaster plan

Disaster here means fire, flood, or other 'act-of-God' that may affect a library. There are two good reasons for creating and maintaining a plan ready to implement immediately should a disaster occur.

Firstly it will assist in maximizing the chances for protection or salvage of the valuable, sometimes unique, materials and the ICT and other equipment, hardware and software that the building contains. Secondly it will provide a framework for maintaining or restoring public services after such a disaster.

The disaster plan will need to both identify the threats and describe the subsequent action necessary.

Potential threats

In considering the potential threats the value of preventative action will become apparent and it may be appropriate to implement some of the preventative action immediately in order to reduce the likelihood or impact of a disaster. In particular the following should be considered:

- the safety and security of the building
- the storage conditions of especially valuable materials
- the possible duplication of irreplaceable or unique holdings by photographic or digital copies
- the need for adequate back-up copies of computer data and storage.

Planning for the emergency

This will involve the compilation of some form of emergency handbook which should:

- describe precautionary measures to be taken in times of known risk
- codify evacuation procedures

- describe salvage procedures
- describe how and what public services will be provided in the event of a disaster
- identify key members of staff and describe their responsibilities should action become necessary
- include a directory of equipment, materials and local contacts for use in emergency.

A member of staff should be designated as having the responsibility for keeping this document up to date.

It will also be necessary to train staff in emergency procedures, to periodically assess insurance cover, and to revisit the terms and conditions under which any special collections have been deposited.

Staffing

6.9 Organizational structure

The information services staffing structure should be designed to:

- manage and operate a cost-effective, quality public information and referral service
- support an integrated information service across the whole of the authority including branches and mobile outlets
- serve to focus professional input for maximum effectiveness since this is the high-cost area of the staff budget
- delineate professional, non-professional and administrative functions, to ensure that tasks are, whenever possible, undertaken with appropriate skills applied and at the right level.

6.10 The manager of the information service

The librarian responsible for the coordination of information services should be on the senior management team. As well as representing the interests of information services in the library's management process, he or she should have a role in determining the overall policies and plans of the service. Subject to the general direction of elected members and senior managers within the authority, and authority policy, the librarian should have the greatest possible freedom of action to develop services in accordance with his or her own professional judgement.

The manager of the reference and information service should be a chartered librarian with appropriate experience.

The manager should be responsible for the following areas:

- development and planning of the services
- budgets and finance
- coordination of information provision within the library authority

- overseeing the appointment of staff
- management of staff and staff training.

Additionally the manager should be:

- closely involved in the provision of information authority-wide
- play a leading role in ICT developments within the authority
- establishing links with other information providers locally, regionally and nationally
- publicizing the resources and services available.

6.11 Information service staffing

Within the reference and information services team there should be appropriately trained and experienced staff available at all times to answer enquiries from users. Sufficient staff should be employed to ensure that no user has to wait more than five minutes for initial assistance. There should also be enough staff to respond promptly to telephone calls, faxes and e-mails, and to assist staff at smaller, less specialist service points within the authority.

Because of the considerable amount of enabling and support work necessary in the provision of an efficient and effective information service, in an ideal situation staff should expect to spend no more than 50% of their time working on an enquiry desk and answering enquiries and the rest of their time on off-desk duties.

The Library Association's *Model statement of standards for public library services* suggests that one-third of library posts should be at professional level. Due to the growth over the last ten years in the number and complexity of enquiries received and the ever increasing range of information sources in a variety of formats, authorities may feel that there should be a higher ratio of professional to non-professional staff in this area. The total professional complement should always be adequate to ensure that full-time professional supervision of the reference and information service is maintained.

Where the service maintains a special collection which may attract visitors and enquiries from outside as well as inside the authority, suitably knowledgeable staff who are capable of meeting the information needs of research workers should be employed.

6.12 Knowledge, skills and competencies required

The Library and Information Commission's report *Building the new library network* identifies four principal roles and functions that all library staff must be able to fulfil. These are the ability to support learning, to provide access to information, to promote reader development and to provide assisted access to remotely delivered public services.

The ability to deliver an effective information service depends on the experience, commitment and skills of the staff. The service needs an adaptable, well motivated and well trained staff, who between them possess the appropriate blend of knowledge, skills and competencies in managerial, technical, professional and specialist disciplines.

The major elements of these requirements are listed below.

- Knowledge is needed on:
  - enquiry technique and the 'reference interview'
  - information retrieval
  - resources available locally and elsewhere
  - interpretation and evaluation of resources
  - identification, selection, management, monitoring and exploitation of sources and services
  - awareness of services and resources of other information providers
  - resource creation and organization
  - assessment, use and exploitation of ICT within the information field.
- Skills are required to:
  - analyse the information needs of existing and potential users
  - develop services to match changing needs
  - interact with staff and users
  - understand patterns of use and barriers to use
  - train and supervize staff
  - train users in use and exploitation of resources
  - communicate with a wide range of people
  - market and promote services.
- Competencies are required to:
  - prioritize tasks and manage time effectively
  - work quickly, accurately and effectively under pressure
  - take a pro-active approach to answering enquiries
  - keep up-to-date with professional developments, trends and best practice
  - undertake work without bias or discrimination.

Training

6.13 Purpose, value and scope

Many of the skills and competencies listed above will be addressed in the authority's general induction and ongoing training programme. However training is needed to help build the more specialized 'knowledge' requirements of the information sector and there are skills and competencies specific to reference and information work that must also be covered.

The staff's approach to the user and their ability to answer an enquiry competently will leave a lasting impression. If the process has been handled well it will encourage the user to return; if it has not the user may be dissuaded from using the service again; and the word will no doubt spread.

Training must be provided for all staff who are required to answer requests for information from the public, whether it is in a large city reference and information service or a small community library. This includes temporary staff, Saturday or Sunday assistants and any staff from other library sections who may work occasionally as relief help.

6.14 Training content

At branch or community library level training should cover:

- the range of information resources held in local library service points
- the use of those materials
- the range and availability of the services and resources of the larger reference and information collections
- enquiry skills
- the use of electronic resources
- the use of ICT equipment.

In a separately staffed reference and information section the training should cover:

- the full range of information resources held in the authority
- the use of those materials
- the range and availability of the services and resources of other information providers locally, regionally and nationally
- enquiry skills
- the use of electronic resources
- the use of ICT equipment
- training users and other staff in information retrieval skills
- promotion and exploitation of the resources and services

In these separately staffed sections staff should not be required to answer enquiries single-handed until they have received full and adequate training. This induction training should include practical exercises, talks from experienced staff and 'shadowing'.

There should be a continuing staff training programme utilizing both internal and external sources. All staff should have their own personal training plan, based on such programmes as The Library Association's CPD, so as to make full use of any opportunities that arise, and this plan should be revised annually in discussions with their manager.

7 Quality of service and performance measurement

Quality

7.1 Defining quality

Many reference and information services state that they aim to provide a high quality information service. But quality is a difficult concept to define and still more difficult to measure.

A user will assess the quality of an information service on the following factors:

- on *tangible* things such as buildings, their decor and layout, and other physical facilities such as equipment
- on the *reliability* of the service in performing the offered service, its dependability and accuracy
- on the *responsiveness* of the service: its willingness to help users and give prompt service
- on the *empathy* shown towards users: the provision of helpful, individual attention
- on the *assurance* a service exudes: its ability to inspire confidence, and show a knowledge of user wants.

7.2 Importance of quality

A balance is required between the quality of service that is affordable and a quality that ensures that the service is well used and cost-effective. Public money should not be wasted on a shoddy product that people do not use; equally a 'Rolls-Royce' service is not the intention of the legislation under which the library service runs.

7.3 Assessment of quality

The draft ISO standard on library performance (ISO/DIS 11620) defines the basic performance criteria for reference and information services, the objective being stated as 'to determine to what extent staff are able to fulfil the primary requirement for a good reference service, namely to provide correct answers to enquiries'. The following section provides a checklist for assessment of this basic requirement.

Performance measurement

7.4 Selection of indicators

Many indicators can be used within a reference and information service to measure performance. The majority of them are quantitative: items in stock, seats, numbers of visitors or enquiries; these are inputs and outputs. Qualitative indicators, gained as a result of questionnaires, interviews, user focus groups, unobtrusive testing, are perhaps more useful at identifying users needs, expectations, experiences and views.

Indicators selected should be measurable, directly related to the service aims and relevant to user needs. Measures should be selected to cover both the efficiency and the effectiveness of the service and to be useful for future planning and development. In other words, it must be possible to use and interpret the information the performance measures reveal.

7.5 Suggested performance indicators

Services and facilities

- hours open
- number of seats available
- number of users per seat provided
- seat occupancy (indication of availability of seats for users)
- number of designated information staff
- ratio of professional to non-professional/support staff
- percentage of time open with professional assistance available
- equipment: range and numbers
- equipment: proportion of time equipment is in use and how long users may need to wait before equipment is available.

Use of service

- visitors in person to library (either by electronic counting or sampling, can include different times of day or in different areas or departments)
- number of telephone calls/fax transmissions/e-mails
- remote uses of library (increasingly important with electronic storage and growth of networks. Can be automatically collected e.g. number of times a database/CD-ROM accessed, length of time in use)
- in-library use of resources (users can be asked not to re-shelve titles after use, these are then counted before being re-shelved by library staff. A more accurate measurement is by random observation at scheduled times and locations – but this is expensive to operate).

Enquiries

Defining and counting enquiries can be difficult and comparisons between authorities can be particularly misleading. The Chartered Institute for Public Finance and Accountancy (CIPFA) defines 'an enquiry' as 'any questions, however received (e.g. in person, by letter, by telephone) leading to the active involvement of staff in identifying and answering problems posed by library users'. On the other hand a 'reference transaction' has been defined by the United States Integrated Post-secondary Education Data System as 'an information contact that involves the knowledge, use recommendations, interpretation, or instruction in the use of one or more information sources by a member of the library staff'.

Performance indicators for enquiries are:

* number of enquiries received
* initial waiting time before an enquiry is handled
* telephone answered within certain number of rings
* letters, e-mails, etc responded to in x days
* materials retrieved from local stores in x minutes
* materials retrieved from out stores in x hours
* user satisfaction (survey to cover timeliness, accuracy, completeness, relevance, helpfulness of staff, amount of information provided)
* needs fulfilled (by unobtrusive monitoring to cover accuracy, completeness and relevance).

Stock

* items added to stock or in stock (may be sub-divided by a number of categories)
* items withdrawn from stock
* annual spend
* periodical titles taken
* proportion of stock on open and closed access (may be reflected in number of enquiries received)
* accuracy of shelving (items in right sections and correct order).

7.6 Users and performance measures

Two important points need to be taken into consideration when expressing and interpreting performance measures. Firstly many indicators do not take into account whether use of the library has been of value to the user. Even when a survey is carried out, the responses depend on the expectations of the users as well as the quality of the service.

Secondly a significant proportion of users of a reference and information service often come from beyond the particular local authority area; they may be commuters, students or researchers. This may create a misleading picture if any findings are expressed per capita of resident population.

7.7   Evaluation

The objective and concrete knowledge gained from performance measurement and assessment can be used to:

- identify and respond to user needs and requirements
- identify shortfalls and achievements
- relate findings to library plans
- manage the service more efficiently and effectively
- monitor progress
- improve parts of the service
- develop an understanding of user expectations
- justify resource allocation
- increase, improve or reallocate resources
- see problems before they arise
- communicate with staff and users
- define the marketing strategy more effectively
- examine the value and impact of the reference and information service.

A well designed programme of performance measures should lead to improvements in the cost-effectiveness and efficiency of the service, and assist in achieving a high quality service. Performance measures can usefully be used to compare the authority with others of the same general type. It is also illuminating to compare present with past performance, either internally or externally.

8 Publicity and promotion

Introduction

It is important that information services maintain a consistently high profile not only within the library service, but also in the local authority, and in the community.

Within the library service this is particularly necessary because of the increased competition for resources within local authorities. The information service must expect to have to argue its case with the rest and must in the first instance persuade and convince the library's management of the value and need for its services.

Within the local authority the same situation applies; also with continuing pressures for increased efficiencies there is a need to cooperate more effectively with other services within local authorities.

Publicity is necessary to maximize the use of the reference and information services and achieve best value from the resources invested. Increasingly sophisticated user expectations are an additional pressure for the service to maintain good visibility within the community.

The maintenance of formal and informal relationships within an authority, with other information providers and with the information industry in general, is covered in Chapter 9. Chapter 1 covers the role of marketing and the use of community profiling and user surveying in getting services right; in this chapter the emphasis is on the publicity and promotion of the services offered.

8.1 General

Publicity and promotion should feature together with marketing as a section of the information strategy. This document should define the target areas for promotional activities and set the standards and methodologies to be used in carrying them out.

8.2 Increasing your visibility

Joint publicity

Reference and information services should be publicized together with the other sections of the library service whenever the opportunity arises. This is important because:

- such publicity will get much wider circulation
- it will automatically reach those who at present do not use the services.

To ensure that the reference and information service has a high visibility in the community:

- make use of all local media; for example staff could offer to write or contribute towards a regular column (business, especially) in the local newspaper, and use local radio
- consider the potential of holding after-hours receptions or other events in the library to highlight specific areas of stock or any new initiatives
- seek commercial sponsorship for specific initiatives, small or large; small donations from local business for single events or openings of services can give both the library service and the donor good publicity
- if the authority has an Internet home page, contribute towards its content, and ensure that the information provided is continuously reviewed and updated
- adopt and adapt marketing ploys used by the commercial sector such as special offers
- look to cooperative ventures with other authorities and other information providers and consider the possibility of constituting a formal group
- take advantage of local or national events
- be aware of outreach or other community activities that branch library staff may be undertaking and try to ensure that relevant information materials are incorporated.

At an operational level:

- assess how effectively the reference and information service is making use of display space both within the library and outside: community notice boards offering free advertising space can be used; paid advertisements in the local media can also be considered
- when there is publicity to send out, use the authority's community profile to target specific groups rather than adopting a blanket coverage approach
- ensure that the reference and information service's publicity materials (flyers, leaflets, bookmarks, etc) remain current and accurate
- ensure that the reference and information service has its own phone number in the local phone books and similar directories.

8.3 First impressions: getting the customer on your side

A user's response to the service starts at the entrance door. Ensure that:

- new or infrequent users can easily make sense of the library's layout
- the enquiry desk is immediately visible from the entrance
- the enquiry desk is staffed and looks welcoming and approachable
- the catalogue is visible, accessible to the public and easy to use
- the signing is effective; for a large library a map may be necessary.

Formal user education

Formal user education activities are costly in terms of staff time and are probably only appropriate for larger services and special groups. They can, however, raise awareness of the service and may save time in the long run if targeted at frequent users, for example adult learners.

Sessions may be appropriate when introducing new services of a technical nature or new collections or types of material, European Union materials for instance.

8.4 Customer feedback and monitoring

This should be used to monitor users' needs and assess the effectiveness of any marketing. Apart from the more traditional surveys (see Chapter 1) a number of other methods can be used:

- Focus groups can be established to enable a selected group of users to meet and discuss the service provided, enabling a constructive interaction with the user base. Such groups either have a finite useful lifetime or the personnel involved will need changing periodically.
- Target groups of specific types of users can be canvassed to assess the effectiveness of certain aspects of the service.
- 'Friends of the Library' or users groups are normally permanent, campaigning groups. By their very nature such groups tend to attract the more vociferous and influential members of the local community, and such people can be very useful allies. Nonetheless, they often need to be directed with care and tact, to avoid them becoming mere social groups or hobby horses.

At the time of writing Government policy encourages a library service to have in place some form of customer comment system. The purpose of this is primarily to make the service more accountable to its users. Advantage should be taken of this requirement and users should be made aware of it. Some sort of system to act upon the comments made is necessary. The system will need to be reviewed periodically to assess its effectiveness and ease of use.

9 Relationships

Introduction

Information service staff should seek to develop links with a wide range of internal bodies and external organizations. This chapter contains guidelines on how this can be achieved within the library service, the local authority and in the wider world. However, whether these relationships are internal or external, they should be regularly reviewed for their actual benefit to the service.

9.1 Within the library service

In order to attract maximum custom it is important that the reference and information service be seen by the public as an integral part of the parent library service. Also, in order to provide information services effectively throughout a library service it is important for the information service to collaborate actively with the rest of the library. Ways of assisting this integration include the manager of the information services being part of the senior management team. All managers should be involved in agreeing priorities for the whole library service.

Responsibility for the provision of reference and information materials and services throughout the library service must be clearly defined. This will lessen problems of funding and staffing of information services outside the main information service points. Also, it should be clearly stated whether the responsibility for children's reference and information material rests with information staff or children's librarians; likewise for all other library services: mobile libraries, housebound services and so on.

It is important that senior information staff play a role in the general management of their library and are involved in meetings, staff selection and other issues.

Information work requires special training and this can make it appear difficult to other staff. It can be helpful to demystify information work by giving all staff, including other professionals, training in enquiry techniques and information resources and moving staff around the library to allow them to develop experience and knowledge in this area. In the same way, information staff can have a better understanding of the pressures facing their colleagues if they spend some time working on lending desks, in children's sections and so on.

In some libraries, there is one main enquiry desk, where staff deal with information enquiries as well as bibliographic requests, registrations, circulation queries and so on. This can encourage members of the public, as well as staff, to take a more rounded view of the libraries' many services.

9.2 Within the local authority

In a well-integrated library service, promotion of the service within the local authority should be a cooperative venture where all sections work together. Internal cooperation involves:

- ensuring that there is an information and reference presence on all appropriate or relevant working parties
- fostering contacts within other departments of the authority
- contributing regular copy to any internal newsletters
- emphasizing by all appropriate means that information and reference services are generally in the forefront of ICT provision within the library service and the authority
- ensuring that the information and reference service takes part in any induction training for new members
- playing a leading role from the outset in any relevant information databases proposed or developed by the authority
- seeking to play a lead role in the authority's information strategy, where it exists
- remembering to keep library staff fully informed and involved: any marketing activities or proposed changes need full staff support as initiatives can succeed or fail on the goodwill of staff in day-to-day contact with users.

Support for the local authority

Support for the local authority can be done on a formal basis. The support provided can take a number of forms.

Some library authorities run an information unit for members and officers of the council. An example might be a local government information unit, based within the authority's headquarters or within a central library. This unit would contain a range of appropriate material, including periodicals and appropriate online facilities, and might have a specialist librarian to answer enquiries and carry out research for members and officers and well as providing information on the council for members of the public.

Current awareness services are provided by some library authorities. A typical example would be a daily abstract of articles from national newspapers which have some relevance to local government issues. Other library authorities might subscribe to this and receive it by fax or e-mail each morning, to circulate to their own members and officers.

A number of library services have taken responsibility for the running of their authority's world wide web site. Even if not taking a lead on such initiatives, information staff should ensure that they are heavily involved at a corporate level in the planning of the council's information strategy.

As a minimum, major reference libraries should promote their own services to members and officers and encourage them to telephone, fax or e-mail with enquiries and requests for material.

Information staff should identify and liaise with information officers from other departments, particularly those with a high public profile and information output such as social services, trading standards, the careers service and education. By developing close relationships with these officers, librarians can build up a picture of the resources held in other departments and can more effectively signpost enquirers to appropriate sources of help.

Library services have increasingly become involved in the provision of information about their council. This is a recognition of the role of the library as shop window for a council and should be encouraged and developed. The role played by services varies: some libraries contain complete 'Council Information Points' or 'one stop shops', with separate enquiry desks, noticeboards and specially trained staff. Others provide space for a terminal that delivers electronic information, or a telephone that is linked to council officers. At its simplest level, council information provision may consist only of a contact list and noticeboard. Whatever the extent of the provision, it is usually managed by reference and information staff and therefore enables the development of a high profile for the service and closer relationships with members and officers in other departments.

Even without a formal 'one stop shop' approach, libraries should provide outlets for leaflets and other material published by the authority. Reference and information staff should ensure that officers in other departments are aware of the network of libraries in the authority and how to get material distributed through them. It is also helpful to promote the library as a venue for displays and surgeries by elected members and by officers from other departments.

9.3 External: professional

By developing close relationships with professional colleagues in neighbouring library authorities, reference and information librarians can stay in touch with new developments and initiatives and share experience and knowledge. This can be particularly valuable when setting up a new service which has already been introduced elsewhere. It is also useful to be aware of the policy of neighbouring authorities with regard to such matters as charges – especially when a library is situated close to authority boundaries, and local residents make use of libraries run by both councils. Professional groups such as The Library Association Information Services Group can be extremely useful here in establishing a forum for information staff to network and exchange news and experiences.

Communication with colleagues from nearby authorities can also lead to cooperation in matters such as the purchase of particularly expensive material and the use of special collections. In particular, some of the small unitary authorities created as a result of local government reorganization can, by liaising with neighbours, extend access for their own users to a much wider range of information material. Training can also be shared with other authorities, cutting costs and encouraging an exchange of knowledge.

It can also be very productive to develop close links with librarians working in local schools and, particularly, colleges of further and higher education and universities.

These links should be extended to cover information providers throughout the area, including those working in government agencies, health authorities and the private sector. It is invaluable to know what special collections are held locally so that the knowledge of expert staff can be drawn on to assist with more specialist and complex enquiries. By exchanging information on resources, such things as union lists of periodicals or Internet bulletin boards can be created and maintained, widening the material available for consultation by the public library user. As wide area networks are developed, it is likely that cooperation of this kind will increase, with resources such as CD-ROMs being shared and networked between a number of different library and information sites.

It is also essential to be aware of and, if possible, make contact with regional and national information providers. Chief amongst these is the British Library, but other valuable sources of information can include national museums and central government offices.

9.4 External: other organizations

There are a wide range of other organizations with which the reference and information service should develop links in order to exchange and share information and refer clients as appropriate. Reference and information staff should ensure that they are on the mailing list for publications produced by these organizations and that they act as distribution outlets for leaflets, posters and so on. Contact should be made with all local clubs and societies for the purpose of gathering community information, and businesses should be aware of special services provided for them. Individual library information staff should be encouraged to form connections with particular groups such as the Citizens Advice Bureau, perhaps serving on management teams to strengthen links.

Examples of specific organizations with which links should be developed are as follows:

- Business Link
- Training and Enterprise Council
- Chamber of Commerce
- youth service
- economic development units
- regional government offices
- Employment Service
- Benefits Agency
- health authority
- Environment Agency
- Rural Development Commission
- archives and records office
- museums services

- police authority
- district, borough, city, town and parish councils
- health information and support agencies (eg drugs, alcohol, AIDS support lines)
- Citizens Advice Bureau
- community education centre
- European Documentation and Information Centres
- Tourist Information Centre and Tourist Board
- local newspaper
- British Red Cross
- Council for Voluntary Service

9.5 Networks

It is useful for the information service to be represented on any appropriate networks that exist in the locality. These might be related to youth issues, training and employment, education, business support, local development or any other community issues. It is important that the library service is recognized to have a key role in providing information and support to individuals and groups in all these fields and, therefore, that it is part of the network.

Information managers in public library services have often been the driving force behind library and information plans (LIPs), which bring together information providers, most usually in a particular geographical area but sometimes within a particular subject field. LIPs can be vehicles not just for networking and exchanging information but for planning the strategic development of cohesive information services. Public library information services can be particularly proactive in establishing links with other sectors such as business and academic institutions for this purpose.

There are various types of information networks. The most common of these include:

- Business information networks, covering the private, public and academic sectors. An example is the southern business information network, Hatrics.
- The Public Information Relay, set up by the European Community to provide information on European matters to the general public through libraries.
- Professional networks covering a particular aspect of library and information development. EARL, for example, is a network of library authorities promoting and developing the use of the Internet in public libraries.

9.6 Partnerships

Libraries and information services in particular need to develop partnerships to provide effective services and avoid duplication. There is increasing pressure to look to sources of external funding for new initiatives and it is almost impossible to access most of these in isolation – evidence of partnership is essential to qual-